To Light a House of Bones

Poems by
Carey Link

BLUE LIGHT PRESS ✦ 1ST WORLD PUBLISHING

1st WORLD
PUBLISHING

SAN FRANCISCO ✦ FAIRFIELD ✦ DELHI

To Light a House of Bones

BLUE LIGHT PRESS
www.bluelightpress.com
bluelightpress@aol.com

1ST WORLD PUBLISHING
PO Box 2211
Fairfield, IA 52556
www.1stworldpublishing.com

BOOK AND COVER DESIGN
Melanie Gendron
melaniegendron999@gmail.com

COVER ART
"Emergence" by Melanie Gendron

AUTHOR PHOTO
Ashley Vaughn
White Rabbit Studios

FIRST EDITION

ISBN: 978-1-4218-3699-7

To Light a House of Bones

For my Mother, Judith Link

Table of Contents

The Cradle of Breeze

Kaleidoscopes bloom from leaves —
sway on a breath
in a cradle of breeze
between earth and sky.

When Branches Bloom

I swing-sway
where infinite colors
bloom from light

on intersected rings
of arcs and hollows —

while shapes of earth and sky
change on ripples
of a breath.

Kaleidoscope

I swing-sway on yellow breeze.
My shadow moves
between the signs and shapes of constellations.

As the mosaic changes,
what color, size, shape,
will the light make me?

A House of Bones

I sit waist-high in a wheelchair.

My head tilts left
and my body curves —
a slanted *S*.

Motion glides
through my hands

as language blooms infinite colors
to light a house of bones.

A House Wren at My Back Door

With pieces of earth and sky on her wings,
she glides through my back door —

turns a circle within a square.

Then her feet rise and fall together
and she rests for a breath

on the round curves
of my blue and white china.

Sezer Raises His Open Hands

Inspired by Leyla Emektar's photograph, Sezer's Diary

In the twilight of afternoon sun,
Sezer sits in his wheelchair,

and waits to catch a basketball
as it glides

back-and-forth — forth-and-back
between earth and sky.

To Come into Being

Beneath the pulse drum
beginnings
of a water cocoon,

you turn concentric circles
waiting to swim
into the palms of my hands —

somewhere between
heartbeat and breath,
darkness and light.

Your first movements
and sounds are flutters.

What colors will light
make your hair,
your eyes?

I Fit in the Palms of Your Hands

At three pounds
I sway in the wings
of your joined hands,
learning to name the colors
and shapes of light.

A Floating Lesson

My hands fit into the center of your palms
as we spin circles together,
on wings made of water —

the only place I can walk.

The Cradle of Our Hands

As you stroke the crooked lines
on the map of my bald head,
the cradle of our joined hands
tethers me to earth.

A Multicolored Head Scarf

My head is a Fortune Teller's map
of intersected veins and bones.

Where a furrowed field waits to grow,
I wear azure,

yellow rose,
orange sun,
and indigo sky

down my back.

Constellations

Inspired by Lee Anne Smith's painting *Trust*

Changing colors of constellations
glide between earth and sky
on a breath of light.

Compass

When I die

I will glide on a curved strand of light
dressed in every color

and sway between earth and sky
on green constellations.

A Knock at My Door

A poem is a knock at my door —
a drop of every color
as silhouettes of dreams intersect

in the cradle of a breath
between earth and sky.

A Measurement of Time

For Bonnie Roberts

You bought your house because of the oak tree
in the front yard,
so you could swing-sway in a hammock
with the arcs and hollows of your childhood
in purple, rose twilight.

When it was struck by lightning,
it fell through time
moved by sky, Earth, and light.

A firefighter was surprised
it didn't crash
through your bedroom window.

Held by the roundness of a breath,
concentric rings on its stump still grow green —
a measurement of time

and a reminder of what is possible
between earth and sky.

A Bridge of Branches

When leaves bloom,
I swing-sway on yellow breeze
through labyrinths of arcs between earth and sky

where I find a red feather
playing hide and seek
and carve my initials in hollows.

What is Found in Arcs and Hollows

A swing between earth and sky
A cradle of knotted green bones
A place for red wings to rest
A compass in a labyrinth
where infinite colors bloom.

Acknowledgements:

I would like to thank Diane Frank for her continued faith my poetry. I am also thankful to Melanie Gendron for her beautiful cover art and design of this book. Finally, I am grateful to Jennifer Horne and Dr. Harry Moore for their endorsements of my book.

"Kaleidoscope" has been previously published in *Conestoga Zen.*

"A Multicolored Scarf" was published in *I Walk a Frayed Tightrope Without a Safety Net* (Finishing Line Press, 2021).

"A House of Bones" is forthcoming in the anthology *Pandemic Puzzle Poems* (Blue Light Press, 2021.)

"To Come Into Being" was previously published in *Awakening to Holes in the Arc of Sun* (Mule on a Ferris Wheel, 2016.)

About the Author

Carey Link lives in Huntsville, Alabama. In 2008, she graduated with a B.A. in psychology from the University of Alabama, Huntsville. Carey is living with Cerebral Palsy. In 2017, two years after developing metastatic breast cancer, she medically retired from sixteen years working in civilian personnel and Equal Employment Opportunity as a civil servant on Redstone Arsenal.

Coping with her disabilities has taught her patience and gratitude. She has never stopped moving forward, and is working toward a Masters in counseling at Faulkner University. After she completes her degree, her goal is to work with clients living with life-altering illnesses and conditions.

Carey's poems have previously appeared in *Birmingham Poetry Review, Hospital Drive, Poem* and elsewhere. In 2011, her chapbook titled, *What it Means to Climb a Tree,* was released by Finishing Line Press; in 2016 her poetry collection *Awakening to Holes in the Arc of Sun* (Mule on a Ferris Wheel, was awarded second place in the Alabama State Poetry Society Book of the Year contest); and in 2020, *Through the Kaleidoscope* was published by Blue Light Press. Her chapbook, *I Walk a Frayed Tightrope Without a Safety Net,* was released by Finishing Line Press in 2021.

Carey enjoys mentoring emerging writers with disabilities through The Handy, Uncapped Pen online program.

9 781421 836997